ELAINE'S
BOOK OF POETRY

Elaine Polk

NEWMAN SPRINGS PUBLISHING
320 Broad Street
Red Bank, NJ 07701

First originally published by Newman Springs Publishing 2021

ISBN 978-1-63881-097-1 (Paperback)
ISBN 978-1-63881-098-8 (Digital)

Printed in the United States of America

ACKNOWLEDGMENTS

To all of my family members who have supported me throughout this endeavor. My siblings have been a few of my biggest supporters.

A special dedication to my husband, Michael, and my daughter, Erica. During this process, they have provided continuous encouragements and support. I believe they can recite these poems better than I can. Thank you for your listening ears.

I cannot leave out all the people of God's ministries who have implored me over the years to write a book. They have provided me with words of wisdom and spiritual food for growth.

Finally, a special dedication to my mother, Corrine Lynch. Her knowledge of the Bible was extraordinary and played a major role in my life. I love you, Mom, and miss you so much.

CONTENTS

Bible Stories We Have Come to Know 7

Psalms 139 8

The Dangers of Pride 10

(Even If You Are Not in Church, Someone Is Always
Watching) The Week I Learned from My Son 12

Can You Imagine? 14

Death Is Defeated 15

My Lovely Card 16

Our Daily Struggles...17

Take a Look Inside 18

The Attributes of a Godly Woman 19

Walk, Walk Away 20

We Appreciate You 21

God's Hospital (The Church)...22

Letting Go Of Issues 24

There Is Power When We Come Together.......................................26

Our Great and Mighty God Can Do Great and Mighty Things ...27

God Can Use Anyone 29

Fighting the Secret Sins 31

God's Special Plan 33

Best Wishes to You..34

The Importance of Testimonials 35

A Birthday Poem to My Sister 36

It's So Hard to Say Goodbye...37

A Praying Mother..38

Are You Properly Covered 39

God Gave You These Birthday Gifts Far, Far in Advance 41

God Understands Our Fears..43

Yes, We Need a Move of God 45

Flowers Just for You...47

The Joy of Music...49

Rise up Ladies, Rise Up...50
I Am…Because of You 51
For God So Loved the World 52
A Church's Dedication 53
The Good Samaritan..54
We Are Living in Perilous Times..................................56
How Strong Is Your Faith?...58
The Call to Lead 60
The Letter 62
The Battered Woman..64
God's Responds (to the Battered Woman) 66

Bible Stories We Have Come to Know

Once there was a woman named Eve;
She was on the brink of being deceived
By the wiles of the devil.
He thought he was clever.
And in the end, his goal was achieved.

Once there was a young lad named David.
His townsfolks were taunted and berated.
So with all that he got,
He took his best shot,
Killed the giant and the people were elated.

Once there was a man named Job.
God considered him perfect and whole.
He was struck with calamities,
Lost members of his family.
God healed him and rewarded him twofold.

Once there was a man named Saul.
He was granted permission to slaughter all
Of the people who were believers
Of Jesus the Redeemer.
But the Lord saved him, and his name became Paul.

PSALMS 139

It is easy to pass judgement
When no one else can really see.
That our own life might be built on
Those same hypocrisies.

We can hide behind the walls
Or a flat computer screen,
Feeling a sense of security
From the fact that we cannot be seen.

But if we look in the Bible
And read Psalms 139;
God knows our every move
And our thoughts at any given time.

The Father knows every word
That proceeds from our tongue,
Whether it is spoken with generosity
Or harmful to someone.

We can try to use the cloak of darkness
To hide away our sins.
Sorry, but that will not work.
It is just like daylight to Him.

Where can we escape?
Where can we flee from His Presence?
He is there if we make our bed in hell
Or if we make our bed in heaven.

So let us ask God to search our hearts
For wickedness and any tests that we are just not passing.
And may He lead us to the way
That is everlasting.

THE DANGERS OF PRIDE

Pride is a dangerous thing,
pure deception in disguise.
It will give you a sense of false bravado
When you feel you are being criticized.
It can make your heart hardened,
Or make you cynical, at best;
When you are confronted with opposition
Or put to a test.

We should be proud of our accomplishments
The goals that we have achieved.
The elation can be overwhelming
When no one else really believed.
We can rejoice in our loved ones' visions
As they reached their ultimate prize.
But the dangers of pride begin
When we start to believe the lies.
Lies that we are far superior,
And do not need anyone else.
Lies that excuses our behavior
And prevent us from seeking forgiveness.
Lies we use to belittle people
Who we deemed not "politically correct."
Lies that we use to ignore the plight of
The poor, homeless, and the neglect.

The Bible repeatedly
Warns us of the dangers of pride.
Open the Book of Proverbs
And take a glimpse inside.
Read the destruction that follows pride;
Taking victims along the way.
Then turn to 1 John chapter 2
and read what it has to say.
So if you want to overcome pride,
There are few things you might do.
Take a long look at yourself
And examine the real you.
This can mean learning to say "I am sorry"
Or practicing humility.
Or better yet, take it to God, our Father,
The Creator of grace and mercy.

(Even If You Are Not in Church, Someone Is Always Watching)

The Week I Learned from My Son

***

On Sunday, I stumped my toe. My young son turned to me.
He said, "Oh, Mommy, you just used profanity."
On Monday, a neighbor wanted bread. I said we are out and closed the door.
My son said, "Oh, Mommy. Remember, you just brought some more."
On Tuesday, I called my job and said that I was sick.
My son said, "Oh, Mommy, we are just stuck in traffic."
On Wednesday, someone asked for my spouse. I said, "I'm sorry. He is not at home."
My son said, "Oh, Mommy, he's upstairs on the phone."
On Thursday, I clipped a car and quickly left the scene.
My son said, "Oh, Mommy, that was very mean."
On Friday, as we were heading to the mall to buy a new dress,
My son said, "Oh, Mommy, you are not supposed to drive and text."

Now, by the time Saturday came,
The last day of the week.
My enthusiasm was gone,
And all I could was weep.

My five-year-old son pointed out things
That I should have known better.
So it was no wonder why I
Had a hard time keeping it together.

Not once did I apologize
To God and my son.
Or to the people that I had wronged.
When all was said and done.

I should have set an example
For my young son to follow.
Now my walk with God
Seems inadequate and shallow.

I must seek God for His mercy.
And pray when tomorrow comes.
That I will have a better week
With my God and with my son.

CAN YOU IMAGINE?

They say a picture is worth a thousand words, then tell me what you see.
When you see a picture of Jesus on the cross, on the hill called Calvary.
Do you see how much He cared for us, the true depths of His love?
That He was willing to sacrifice His life, willing to shed His blood.

Do you see the numerous stripes that showed
how His flesh was cut like meat?
A punishment so cruel to one who had no guile or deceit?
Do you see His head dripping with blood because of the thorny crown?
Oh, the pain that He endured when He could have easily stepped down.

Can you imagine the nails that were pounded
in His feet and His hands?
The sounds of heavy hammers reverberating across the land?
Can you imagine being mocked and spat
upon while in the throes of death?
Can you imagine His mother watching on as
He was taking His final breath?

Just imagine before He gave up the ghost, He asked the Father to forgive
All the participants, the soldiers, the ones
who did not want Him to live.
Can you imagine one of those same soldiers still pierced His side.
But by then, Jesus Christ had already died.

This gory picture depicts a love story that most of us have read.
But the ending was remarkable; three days
later, Christ rose from the dead.
The King of Kings, Lord of Lords, Our Redeemer
who loved Gentiles and Jews.
And everything He experienced was for me and for you.

DEATH IS DEFEATED

He rides in as if on a horse
To snatch his next prey.
The unsuspecting victim does not
Realize this will be his last day.

This unmerciful beast
Takes the young as well as the old.
Although he kills the body
He would rather have the soul.

But death's end is coming.
He knows that he has lost.
For Jesus Christ sealed his fate
The day He died on the cross.

When Jesus Christ rose again,
He rescued you and me.
O death, O grave!
Where is thy victory?

For that day will surely come
In the twinkling of an eye.
The trumpet will sound
And the dead shall arise.

We will go to a land with milk and honey;
The streets are paved with gold.
All because Death took our body,
But he could not destroy our soul.

MY LOVELY CARD

The gifts you gave me were beautiful.
It touched me to the core.
And if it was at all possible,
They made me love you more.

Not just because they were wonderful;
Though I love every one of them too.
But it is the card that was so personal,
As if it was written by you.

Each word was so poignant.
It reduced me down to tears.
It described the love that we still have;
After marriage of 25 years.

Truly God has blessed our union.
We kept Him first in our lives.
And I have never regretted the phrase I do;
That day I became your wife.

OUR DAILY STRUGGLES

The daily struggles in life
Have a way of sapping our strength.
As soon as we overcome one,
Then another becomes more intense.

We may try to control our demeanor.
And not let our problems weigh us down.
But that is far easier said than done
When we are constantly losing ground.

But this is when God shows up
And intercedes on our behalf.
The extent of His awesome powers
Are more than minds can grasp.

For we know with Him, nothing is impossible.
He can just speak them all away.
But if He took away all our struggles
Do you think we would have reasons to pray?

So if we wait upon the Lord,
He will renew our strength.
We shall mount up with wings as eagles
And run any length.

We will not be weary or faint.
God's promises are written in stone.
So as we struggle, we must remember
He will never leave us alone.

TAKE A LOOK INSIDE

There is a strange thing that is happening;
I wish someone would explain it to me.
How can so many people wish harm on others
While practicing Christianity?

This phenomenon used to be subtle,
Done with a wink and a nod.
But that is no longer the case;
The quiet part is said out loud.

Where is the love that Jesus spoke of?
That He emphasized in His talks.
That same love that showed grace and mercy for others
While He was on a sea and as He walked?

What ever happened to loving your neighbors?
The Bible did not speak of any exception.
Could it be that we all are caught up
In some diabolical deception?

Whatever is happening, this is
Something that we should address.
For it is causing pure vitriol, evilness,
And a bunch of anguish.

But our first step toward healing
Begins with looking at ourselves.
Then maybe we can truly learn
To love everyone else.

THE ATTRIBUTES OF A GODLY WOMAN

The attributes of a godly woman
Are beautiful qualities to view.
As she goes about her routine
With earnest and quiet dignity too.

Strength and honor are her clothing.
Her shoes; the preparation of the gospel.
Her offspring are spiritual fruits
Spoken of by Paul the great apostle.

There we meet goodness, love, and joy,
Along with meekness and temperance.
Longsuffering is also present
To increase her endurance.

For she is not exempt from life's struggles.
No, what is more crucial is how she handles them.
As her life becomes an example
For women who have their own share of problems.

So, ladies, if you are seeking
Someone to mimic today.
Get connected to a godly woman
That is living the godly way.

WALK, WALK AWAY

Temptation is all 'round us.
A good remedy is to pray.
But one of the easiest escape
Is to walk, walk away.

You might feel at that moment.
It is your perfect chance to say
That they were wrong, and you were right.
But walk, walk away.

An old crush might approach you.
And now he wants to play.
But you are saved and married.
So just walk, walk away.

You are confronted by some haters.
Who said spiteful things today.
I don't know, but this might be the time
That you seek God and pray.

For the Word says, there is no temptation taken us.
But such as is common to man.
But God is faithful and will make an escape
So that we will be able to stand.
So when you see temptation around you,
And you might be lured away.
Take heed and follow my advice!
And walk, walk away.

WE APPRECIATE YOU

We are here to honor you, our Pastor, friend, our leader.
Truly it would be hard to find another who is
more compassionate, kind or sweeter.
For you have exemplified Christ in everything you do
That is why we like to say, we appreciate you.

You have this gift of inspiration; we watched it over the years.
As you encouraged those around you despite their doubts or fears,
You shared in some of our weddings, our
births. And even in moments of grief,
You were there to whisper words of comfort as we sat in disbelief.

You listen to our problems as we deal with constant pressure.
Yet confident are we that they will not be the
topic of your next Sunday's lectures.
And still we call on you at all hours of the day.
But you would say come and take my
hands; it is time for us to pray.

It is those same hands that are always open to welcome one and all.
No one is too great, and no one is too small.
So you see, these are just few of the reasons
that we are happy to have a part
In showing our appreciation for you, for you
have touched each one of our hearts.

God's Hospital (The Church)

Welcome to God's hospital
Those of you who are sick, battered, or just tired
Here, there is no long forms to fill out
No registration is required
No insurance cards are needed
The cost has already been paid
To cover any wrongdoing, bad decisions
And all mistakes that you have made
The Doctor is always on duty here
And He is waiting just for you
To connect you to His bloodline
And purge you through and through
His healing powers are awesome
Just ask the person sitting beside you
His mission statements are available
They are written in the Good Book to guide you
The Doctor's reputation is impeccable
He is known all over the world
He has treated people of all ages
Men, women, boys, and girls
He can make the lame to walk, the blind to see
He can even raise up the dead
He can make the mountains move or the rocks to cry out
But He will rather use us instead
So if you hear somebody cry
And begin to dance around
Don't worry…a transformation has taken over
God is placing them on higher ground

This change can happen swiftly
Or it may take a little more time
But the peace that follows afterward
Is unexplainable yet sublime
So come all of you who are brokenhearted
Distressed or you have just lost your way
God's doors are always open
Won't you give Him a try today?

Letting Go Of Issues

How often in life do we let situations dictate what we should be?
Or perhaps we listen to others to define our destiny
But those same people are quick to remind
us of what we did in the past
They will watch and wait to see how long our change will last.
We all know Satan's job is to steal, kill, and destroy
He will bring up our past to try and rob us of all our joy.
He will remind us that our father, mother,
or a loved one was not there
Or how we are struggling to survive, and no one really cares.
But we, too, will hang on to things that do not edify our spirits.
Like certain Facebook posts, TV shows, or music with explicit lyrics.
We will hang on to our children when they don't want to be saved,
Trying to fix their problems when they know how to behave.

We will hang on to old habits that never seems to die.
Oops, I mean maybe they would if we would just only try.
Maybe one of you is fighting a battle that is not even yours;
Got you so mad and upset you feel like opening up a Coors.
We will hang on to these issues and more
like they are monkeys on our backs,
And before you know it, we are out of God's
will and off His chosen tracks.
So I am telling you today while we are all gathered here,
It is time to let go of our guilt, hurts, anger, and fears.
Remember, there is nothing more important
that saving your own soul,
Forgetting the former things nor consider the things of old.
The world may think that they have something
on us, but we have something greater

No one can take it away and that is Jesus Christ, our Savior.
His endless love, grace, and mercy can cover a multitude of sins
So forget them and let them all go, and
He will give you peace within.

There Is Power When
We Come Together

We are here for Family and Friends' Day,
so we all should be excited.
Regardless of what church we attend, in Christ we stand united.
For there is nothing more powerful than
when we all get on one accord
And release those things that are holding us
down and start praising the Lord.

You see, this is evident in the Bible, like in Psalms 34:3.
David says, let us exalt His name together,
magnifying the Lord with me.
Look at Hebrews 10:25, the Word says let us exhort one another.
With specific instructions to include the
assemblance of ourselves together.

Let us read Acts chapter 2 about the day of Pentecost,
How the Holy Word was sent forth and
saved thousands that were lost.
What about Galatians 6:2. It says we shall bear each other's burdens.
But, at times, we get so caught up that we
forget the folks who are hurting.

Consider this:

If one can chase a thousand and two can chase much more,
Imagine if half the churches came together
the things God would have in store.
I can go on and on about this, but in closing I will just say.
Thank you one and all for coming out on
our Family and Friends' Day.

OUR GREAT AND MIGHTY GOD CAN DO GREAT AND MIGHTY THINGS

God has made us many promises that they are hard to absorb
The significance of what they all mean,
the power behind His Words.
But in Jeremiah 33:3, the Lord has declared
That if we would just open our mouth and
call on Him, He would be right there.
To show us great and mighty things that we cannot understand.
Things hidden, unrecognizable, things not known to man.
While the carnal man places limits on God
and cannot see beyond the realm,
The spiritual man acknowledges God's
power, for He is the great I Am.

For who else can throw the stars up to the
sky and name them one by one?
Or stop the flow of the raging sea or control the moon and sun?
Who else can open the wombs of barren
women way beyond their prime?
Or clench the mouths of angry lions to save their men just in time?
Tell me, who else can just speak to make the
blind to see or even the lame to walk?
Or change the course of speeding bullets
to make them miss their marks?
Who else can change the drunk, the addict, the harlot, the sick,
the lying, the poor and make them the head and not the tail?
Who else can do anything, anything at all, who else can never fail?

Well, this same great and mighty God is waiting to hear from you.
To show you anything is possible no matter what man may do.
If God said He will do it; He will do it indeed;
for redemption is offered to all.
But even greater promises are given to those
who has repented and becomes the call.

GOD CAN USE ANYONE

God's plans for you were not known to many
when you stepped out on faith one day
For you have heard the sound of Jesus's
voice and said, "Lord, I will obey."
So you started out with your members who had the
same faith and the right kind of chemistry
And thus began the origin of *The Redeemed
of the Lord Outreach Ministry*.

It did not take long for tongues to wag or
for doubters to begin to chime in.
They said, "Hey, we know what she used to
do, the places that she has been."
It seems they didn't know the verse God's ways are not
our ways, His thoughts are not our thoughts.
For Pastor T., God knew what you would be before
you were born despite the habits and faults.

Ant it was because of those old habits, God
needed you to go back out into the streets,
To tell the young women and tell the young
men they don't have to accept defeat.
For all the mistakes that they have made,
Jesus Christ has borne the stripes
So they no longer have to sell their bodies or hustle day or night.

And yes, it was because of your old sins God
wanted you to witness to the lonely,
To aid the sick, comfort the bereaved,
and feed the poor and hungry.
For what could be more powerful to see than one
who has been down in the dirt and mud,
And now is redeemed and washed clean
by the shedding of Jesus's blood.

God's plan for you is far from over, even though
you don't dot every i's or cross all t's.
But He sees you still crying out to Him
every night on bended knees.
So remain steadfast, be strong. There are more people
that need to be saved, encouraged, and taught
That God can use anyone despite their old habits and faults.

Fighting the Secret Sins

As Christians, we fight an internal battle.
There is no need for us to hide it.
But what is so amazing about our battle,
the winner is already decided.
For as long as we walk earnestly with the Lord
And arm ourselves accordingly using our Bible as our sword.
In Romans chapter 7, Paul reminded us of this feat.
He wrote when he wanted to do right, he did
wrong; but he did not give up in defeat.
Paul recognized that his wretched body was full of sins and desires.
And only God could deliver him so that he could go higher.
Like Paul, we too must realize the sins that lie deep within.
We can jump, shout, dance, preach, and even try to pretend.
But there is a dark inner being that wants to gain control.
The consequences are dire; the results could be our soul.
Now that we know the fight is on, I thought
I would ask a few questions
So that we could be honest with ourselves and
bring our bodies under subjections.
These questions may seem irrelevant, but they could be a start
To change the way we think and change our wayward hearts.

Do you become jealous or embittered by someone's else success?
Do you thrive in confusion or delight in others' mess?
Are you hoping for a certain individual to fail?
Do you laugh and spread the news when a fellow member post bail?
Do you find it hard to guard your tongue
and you don't know what to say?
Especially when you are wronged and things do not go your way?

What about when you are mad, do you pray
or do you find yourself instead,
Saying the first unfiltered thing that seems to pop inside your head?
Do you judge people on how they act or what they decide to wear?
By nudging your neighbors and giving them
that "oh no, they didn't glare"?
Are you quick to point out the faults of
others but fail to see your own?
Forgetting that there is One who sees all
while sitting on His throne.
Do you look down on others because of their status, color, or creed?
Do you close your fists up tight when you see a member in need?
Is it hard to say I am sorry because your pride gets in the way?
Do you hold on to yesteryears' grudges
as if they had occurred today?
Do you only go to church to be seen, heard, or mingle?
Looking for a mate who may be married but unhappy, or single?
Are you obedient to the one that God has placed over you?
Do you murmur and complain when she
gives you something to do?

● ●

Our secret sins can show up in all manners, ways, and forms
And become quite dangerous when we justify
them and accept them for the norm.
But from Genesis through Revelation, we
can find our strength anew.
With a passage here and a passage there, instructing us what to do.
If we combine that with prayers, fasting, and
supplications to help overcome our fight,
The fight in you, the fight in me; we can declare victory tonight.

God's Special Plan

God had a special plan for you even before you were conceived.
He knew the places you would go, the roads you
would take, the things you would achieve.
By the time that you were born, the wheels were already in motion.
And God, whose work is never done, set
aside your reasonable portion.
For He had assigned you specific tasks that
few folks could have only imagined.
You confided in some, and they told others,
who believed it would not happen.
Like Joseph, you heard their scorn, yet you refused to be held down.
For you knew that God could take the impossible
things and turn them all around.

So like Abraham, nine years ago, you set out on your own.
To build your church on the Holy Word
with Jesus as the cornerstone.
And like Job, you patiently waited to see
the fruits of some of your labor.
Then when you became blessed, you turned
around to bless your friends and neighbors.
So it is no wonder why we are here today. You
have touched each one of our lives.
Your love for God is extraordinaire, and it teaches us how to survive.
Now as you continue to carry out His special
plans, we pray that you remain blessed.
And may all the days of your life be filled
with joy, peace, love, and happiness.

BEST WISHES TO YOU

I glimpse a future bright for you
That promises dreams unspoken
With plenty of colors splashing your life
Symbolical and as a token
Of things to come. If you pursue them
Earnestly in faith
No matter how hard the fight
No matter how long the wait
You have the gift of inspiration
Just breathe them into life
Continue to pour out your soul
And continue also to write
Write about the good times
And yes, write also about the bad ones
For they will bring you knowledge
And prepare you of things to come
And if you shall stumble,
Remember we all do at times
Often God can only get our attention
When we are flat on our behind
Take Him along as your companion
He will be your special friend
For no matter who walks this journey with you
God will be there until the end
And even though our paths crossed
How briefly it may be
I shall always remember you
You have a friend in me

THE IMPORTANCE OF
TESTIMONIALS

Testimonials are evidence of God's mercy and His grace
To show that He is with us no matter what obstacles we face.
There are no age restrictions; the young and old can stand
And tell how God reached down from heaven to give us a hand.
We all should say something though. He has no respect of persons;
His love is the same for those in the church and
those on the street corners cursing.
Just a simple phrase of thanks can open up His ears;
An outstretched hand, a song of praise, or a face filled with tears.
However, testifying is not a time to boast or exaggerate,
To make what you are saying sound
believable, incredulous, and great.
It is time to reflect on how often we have been blessed.
So that our words of victory can help someone else.

Now let us just stop and think about this for a brief second or two
And recall some of the things that God
may have brought us through;
Like sicknesses, diseases, addictions, and hurt
Scheming, betrayals, our name dragged through the dirt
Homelessness, abandonment, periods in jail
Domestic abuse which caused our relationships to fail.
BUT WAIT!
Our stories are not over; there is work to be done.
Look around this city; there are souls to be won.
So let us open our mouth and give God His glory.
It is because of Him we are able to tell our amazing stories.

A Birthday Poem to My Sister

On September 13, I won't say the year, God saw that it was time
For you to carry out His plans, that He had thoughtfully designed.
I imagined that you came out kicking and
screaming as if ready to take on the world.
And God, perhaps with a smile on His face, might
have said not now my precious girl.
For His plans required strategic timing to bring you into the open;
For a mission to call all the sick and the lost,
and those who spirits were broken.
Ooh, this wouldn't be a task for the faint at heart;
God knew it would require strength.
For the roads would be bumpy, the nights so
long, and the battles quite intense.

So God molded you and nurtured you. His hands were on your life;
During times of happiness, during times of heartaches and strife.
And at various stages, He secured your armor
to block what was to come.
He deflected thousands of fiery darts, but He
allowed you to be hit with some.
Yet look at you today; a strong mother, a Pastor
who is still on fire for the Lord!
Unmovable, anointed woman of God, still preaching His Holy Word.
We don't know what else God has in store for
you, but we are glad to have a part
In celebrating this special moment with you, for
you have touched each one of our hearts.

It's So Hard to Say Goodbye

The time is fast approaching
When we must say goodbye.
It is hard to ignore the pain,
It is hard not to cry.

For I know you have made a vow
To protect the USA
A duty you must perform
Even though I want you to stay.

My days will be filled with agony.
My nights will be ever so long.
Yet, I see the love you have for our country.
So, I must try to remain strong.

But I hope you carry with you
This message loud and clear.
No matter how many miles that are between us,
I will always love you, dear.

A PRAYING MOTHER

God had a special plan for me even before I was conceived.
My mother would tell me this all the time, but I never did believe.
She said God would reveal it in His own time one day.
I would laugh and wave her off, but she continued to pray.

She prayed and fasted for all her kids as I soon discovered.
She would say I have to pray even harder each time we got into trouble.
At times, I often marveled at her unwavering faith,
As I observed this single mother with so much on her plate.

But she was tapped into a source of power I had yet to understand.
It did not come from money, or possessions; it did not come from man
What she possessed was something far, far greater
That only could be obtained through Jesus Christ, her Savior.

Even though she is no longer here, she knew without a doubt
That God's Words would not come back void. His plans would be carried
out.
Now as I see His plans for me being revealed more and more each day,
I thank God for a mother that certainly knew how to pray.

DEDICATED TO CDL

ARE YOU PROPERLY COVERED

"He that dwelleth in the secret place of the most High shall abide under the shadow of the Almighty" (Psalms 91:1).

There are various types of coverings that are essential in your lives.
Some serve as basic functions, while others are tools to survive.
For example, our wardrobe is a type of covering that keeps us from being exposed.
From insect bites, prying eyes, the extreme heat or bitter cold.

There is coverage with insurance to protect us from the unknown.
Good coverage can help with the costs of burial plots, rental costs, or the loss of our home.
But the coverage that God provides is more valuable than these.
The vastness of His protection is shrouded in mysteries.

Yet, under the umbrella of His covering there is safety within.
This protection goes into effect once we have repented of our sins.
Our position is very important; we must remain under His shadow.
And watch the Lord go to work and fight our continuous battle.

With His feathers, He can block the pestilence that comes around at night.
Casting away the destruction in the dawning of the light.
1, 2, 100, 1,000 shall all fall at our side.
Although the number may increase to 10,000 or more, we have no reason to hide.

For God is our refuge, our strength, a very present help in trouble.
In time, He may give us all that we have lost or even reward us with double.
We are living in an age where there is so much destruction, hatred, pain, and sufferings.
So now is not the time we should be caught without our proper spiritual covering.

So, stay covered

GOD GAVE YOU THESE BIRTHDAY GIFTS FAR, FAR IN ADVANCE

We are here to celebrate your birthday today.
You will probably get presents galore,
But nothing can compare to the ones
that God already had in stored.
For He instilled in you certain gifts
that have made you different from the rest.
Gifts that left many folks baffled,
but few knew you were blessed.

For God gave you the gift of wisdom; like Ruth
who knew that God would provide a way,
The faithfulness; like Hannah whose solution to everything was pray,
God instilled in you integrity; like Deborah as she ruled over the land,
And the courage; like Queen Esther who saved her people from Haman.

God instilled in you humility; like Martha
whose delight was to wait on others,
And the cleverness; like Miriam as she schemed
to keep her family together.
God gave you a giving spirit; like Dorcas, who
passed out garments to her friends,
And the quiet strength; like Mary who walked with Jesus to the end.

And if that was not enough…

God provided you a helpmeet,
so that you both could be on one accord
As you build up treasures here on earth
and the Kingdom of the Lord.
This helpmeet will hold you up,
if ever you shall bend.
For he promised to be with you
through times of thick and thin.
So, as we celebrate your birthday today,
remember whenever you get a chance,
That God gave you these birthday gifts far, far in advance.

GOD UNDERSTANDS OUR FEARS

Fear is defined as an anxiety disorder
That affects people of all age, gender, status, and color
But if it is left unchecked, its roots can stretch deep and wide
Until it chokes off the good we might feel inside
(We must first understand that)
Most fears are borne out of distrust and concerns
From the things that we have observed to
the things that we have learned
We may try to act strong and put on a façade
But one thing I know is we cannot fool God
For the all-knowing God sees just what we need
Like when He saw Abram's desire for a future seed
So, God said, "Fear not. I am thy shield. I got you, my son
Your seed will be innumerable when it is all said and done
I will give you a land for you to possess
Just follow my lead and I will do the rest."

And so, throughout the Bible, God continued to console His people
As He saw their struggles, their fears, their constant upheavals
In Joshua 1:9 God said, "Do not be dismayed
I am always with you. There is no need to be afraid."
And if we look through Exodus and at Isaiah 41:10
The same message is repeated over and over again
But God added, "I will strengthen you
with the use of my right hand
And I will confuse your enemies; there is no need to fear man."

You do not have to lift a finger; the Lord will fight your battle
And the number of your enemies will not even matter
If He did it for Moses, Gideon, and Jehoshaphat too
God knows your name; He will do it for you
For our names are inscribed on the palms of His hands
So, God sees when we fall, and He sees when we stand
The Lord sees all our struggles. He sees all of our fears
He sees all our sorrows. He sees all of our tears
He will bottle them up along with His own
His compassion fails not even when we do wrong
Oh, what a mighty God we really do serve
He gives us what we need; not what we deserve
We many never understand the whole picture, but one thing is clear
God is working behind the scenes to address all of our fears

Yes, We Need a Move of God

If we look at the state of the world today,
it's easy to become discouraged.
People, filled with hate in their hearts,
don't care who they disparaged.
They spread their prejudices and their lies
using various media platforms.
With little regards to the impact they would
have or the people that they could harm.
Meanwhile, drugs and guns are more accessible
than the medicine for the sick.
It's no wonder we're experiencing massive
shootings, and the rise of opiate epidemic.
The cost of living has risen so fast; people
are living on streets and in cars,
Forcing some to seek comfort in the arms
of others, or in clubs, and in bars.
Ironically, it's been said, that the church doors
are always open to welcome one and all.
But sometimes the visitors leave more confused,
feeling so helpless and small.
For the Word preached is often focused,
on how entirely one is dressed.
Forgetting the main purpose is to bring them
in and let Jesus Christ do the rest.
And, we as Christians, we've become bogged
down too; our growth at times stagnant,
From holding on to issues in our lives, as if
they were some sort of magnets.
Our prayer's life decreases, our fasting sporadic,
our faith weeble and wooble.

We forget that God has given us authority as well as given us power;
Power to tread on serpents and scorpions, power over all our foes,
Power to heal the sick and the lost. Power wherever we go.
So, yes, we need a move of God to heal and restore us today.
Yes, we need a move of God. Lord, hear us now we pray.

FLOWERS JUST FOR YOU

Too often in life, we say the most beautiful things
about people that are no longer here.
We recall the joy, the love, and the memories
that we hold so precious and dear,
But it's with great pleasure that we are here
today to give honor where honor is due
To someone who is alive and well, so Pastor
V, here are some flowers for you.
Like most mothers, you've made numerous sacrifices;
the half of which may have never been told
To ensure that your children were provided for;
to make them well-rounded and whole,
You encouraged individuality. You laid the groundwork for their success.
You taught them to always go for their dreams,
and never settle for anything less.

Like most wives, you cherish your husband.
The two of you are on the same accord
As you build up your treasures here on the
earth and the Kingdom of the Lord.
The respect that you have for one another is such a delight to see.
It only confirms the words that are written in
the 3rd Chapter of Amos Verse 3,
And like most true friends, your support is
invaluable. We thank God for you every day
For you are always available to lend a hand in a variety of ways.
We often seek your advice; and yes, there are times we don't always agree,
Yet we know that your words are spoken out
of love, compassion, and sincerity.

But your most important role is that of a pastor,
you are an effective leader. That's true.
Many people can speak the Word of God, but
we see Him living through you.
You encourage us to grow, to read the Word,
to develop a one-one with God.
You remind us to fast and pray, to endure the
race even when times seem hard.
So, what better way is there to honor you than
on your special day of the year,
A day that should bring you plenty of blessings,
joy, and lots of good cheers.
These "flowers" are just symbols of who you are
and about some of the things that you do,
But they are also our way of saying thank you, we
love you, and a very happy birthday to you.

The Joy of Music

Music plays an intrinsic part of our life.
It can make us smile or even cry
As we reflect on our current circumstances,
Or reflect on days gone by.

Sometimes words are not necessary
To get a reaction or two.
Just listening to the instrumental versions
Can even do something to you.

For many decades, secular music
Dominated the industries.
With artists like, Aretha, Elvis, and Diana Ross,
Could sing songs that make you fall to your knees.

But good old gospel music is also sentimental.
It, too, can lift your spirits.
Especially when one of your favorite artists
Began singing the heartfelt lyrics.

So, if you want to do some throwback
While retreating to your quiet place,
Just listen to one of these well-known artists,
Crooned to the sounds of Amazing Grace.

Rise up Ladies, Rise Up

For many centuries, the men were the only leaders of church.
Their position of prominence was based
on where they were perched.
Over time, something happened. What? I really do not know.
But where did all the young and old men go?

Somewhere they have gotten sidetracked and dropped the baton.
Ladies, you know, God's work must go on.
He will use whatever, whomever He pleases
To get us to call on the Name of Jesus.

We, too, have gotten complacent; idle at times.
On fire in the beginning, now sitting on our behind.
Our thirst has diminished, our hunger abated.
Instead of excitement, we have become frustrated.

We have forgotten there are people hurting, hungry and cold;
Desperate, rude, and angry, but they still have souls.
So, let us rise up ladies, rise up and see
The work that God has intended for you and for me.

I Am ... Because of You

If my family look at me and see
A reflection of what I used to be,
Confounded by my new maturity
I am...because of you.

If my friends desert me in the upcoming days,
Perplexed by my changing ways,
All because I give God praise
I am...because of you.

If a stranger shall see my light,
Amazed because it shines so bright,
Not knowing how I have endured the fight,
I am...because of you.

For as a child you have guided me,
And taught me to have respect and humility,
While warning me of the price of iniquity,
I am...because of you.

Now here I stand, proud to be your son
As I reach out to help someone,
Hoping one day God will say a job well done
I can...because of you.

Written by EDP
Dedicated to Charlotte Polk
From: Michael Polk

For God So Loved the World

For God so loved the world
That He gave His only Begotten Son
To die for you, to die for me
To die for everyone.
Our skin tone does not matter,
Nor the zip code where we live
Only that we accept Him as our Savior
And our sins He will forgive.

He will forgive the local drunk and addict
Who walks up and down the street
The prostitutes who proposition
the people that they meet
He will forgive the prodigal children
who have yet to return home
the mothers who have released their children
before they were even born.

God will forgive the abusive men
Who lash out on their wives
The people who use illegal methods
In order to survive
He will forgive the loose tongues and gossipers
Who spread more lies than truths
And those who hold leadership roles
To prey upon the youth.

This awesome God will forgive almost anything
Let us invite Him in our hearts today
Then feel the peace that surpasses all understanding
Melt our darkness away.

A Church's Dedication

Welcome to the International House of Worship
Where the Lord reign Supreme,
Where the lost and the rejected can enter in,
And leave restored and redeemed.

Our mission is pure and simple,
And that is to win souls for the Lord.
Timeout for the traditional religious norms
It's time for God's people to get on one accord.

With Pastor E. at the helm
And co-Pastor T. at her side,
Together they preach the Holy Word
And that's Jesus Christ glorified.

The stewards are in position
That include the elders, deacons, and ministers too.
Here, everyone has a purpose
Every member has a job to do.

We're expecting God to do great things
For He is not a man that He should lie.
God has made over 7,000 promises
Some of them have yet to materialize.

So, let us enter into His gates with thanksgiving,
And enter His courts with praise.
Stay tuned and watch God go to work
We are sure you'll be amazed.

The Good Samaritan

When he saw me in the corner,
He did not look at my clothes.
They were crumpled and filthy,
And my shoes were full of holes.
My odor was overwhelming
By the look on his face.
But he grabbed my hand and pulled me up,
And said let us leave this place.
I was too scared to even move
And too weak to resist.
After hours of being kicked,
I tensed up for the next few hits.
He offered up soothing words.
They were like balm to my soul.
With no further resistance,
I did like I was told.

He led me to a diner
And ordered us some food.
I gobbled it up oh, so fast.
I have never tasted anything quite this good.
No other words were spoken,
Yet the tears freely flowed.
Then he gave a great big smile
I guess my face somehow showed
The gratitude that I felt
That came not with a price.
It has been a long time coming
Since someone has treated me nice.
It did not matter that I was homeless.
My appearance was overlooked.

Then he shoved some money in my hands
Along with a card and book.
He left without a word,
But I still felt good inside.
I was determined to start afresh
After I had one last good cry.
I flipped the book around.
I knew what I would see.
It was the King James Holy Bible
That spoke of life eternally.
The card belonged to a counselor
Who help people on heroin.
But at this moment I am so grateful
For my good Samaritan.

WE ARE LIVING IN PERILOUS TIMES

You know that we are living in perilous
times when children of all ages
Are being separated from their parents and locked into steel cages.
Spectators laugh with glee while politicians clap their hands
Hoping this very action will make America great again.

You know that we are living in perilous times
when natural disasters kill thousands.
Hundreds of families are displaced and left
without adequate food or housings.
Meanwhile, wars are all around us, and
countries are constantly sending
Troops over here and troops over there, with
no signs of them ever ending.

You know that we are living in perilous times when
men have become lovers of themselves.
Blasphemous, boasters unholy; with little respect for anyone else.
Their loyalty is conditional, just don't say or do anything wrong,
For the moment will come when you look for
them you will find out you are all alone.

You know that we are living in perilous times
when the church is devoid of love
Having a form of godliness but lacking the powers thereof.
The church used to be a sacred place where
we could don our very best
What it looks like what we really need now is access to Kevlar vests.

But through it all, I'll still fight the good fight of faith
For I know what God has done for me.
He picked me up out of the miry clay,
And saved and set me free.

And I'll still fight the good fight of faith
For I saw a mother dancing
Giving praise to God Almighty,
Even as she was battling cancer.

And I'll still fight the good fight of faith
For I have read the book of Revelation.
Satan's rule will come to an end,
And God will raise up His Holy Nation.

HOW STRONG IS YOUR FAITH?

The Bible says without faith, it is impossible to please God.
We quote this scripture so many times, but are we just a fraud?
We claim that we trust God as things are going great;
Our health is good, our bills are paid, and
we have food on our plates.
But what about those times when our future seems unknown?
Our health is declining, we have lost our
jobs, and possibly our home.
Does our faith take a hit or two and slowly starts to waver?
Do we call on everyone else but Jesus Christ, our Savior?

Has our faith become like Simon Peter while
he walked on the water toward Christ?
He started off strong, became unfocused, and almost paid the price.
Or is our faith like doubting Thomas,
who had to see, touch, and feel?
Just to believe that Jesus' resurrection was truly real.
Maybe our faith is like Gideon. He asked God to complete two tests
In order to believe on God's Words and put his fears to rest.
Perhaps our faith is like Jeremiah, a.k.a. the weeping prophet.
Depression often swallowed him up and it
seemed he just could not stop it.
For certain, we would want the faith like the
woman who had the issue of blood for years.
She knew she had to do whatever it took
for Jesus of Nazareth was near.
How about that faith like Abraham who almost sacrificed his son?
He did not see a ram in the bush, but he
hoped that God would provide one.

Wherever our faith lies at this very moment,
one thing is certainly true.
As long as we are in the land of the living,
we are going to go through.
Be it disappointments, heartaches, and the decline of our health,
Family separations, hardships, and yes, even death.
There is no way around this; even money has its limit.
No physic hotline we can call or any man-made gimmicks.
The secret is we must hold on to our faith as we endure this race.
Until that day will arrive when we see Jesus face to face.

THE CALL TO LEAD

*Not so long ago, God breathed a breath of
life and a tiny seed was formed.
This child was destined to preach against
the traditional religious norms.
Of course, she would not know that; so, God would just carry her along
Until the day would arrive when she would become battle strong.
God watched over her with love as she advanced through the years.
He smiled when she laughed; He groaned when she shed tears.
He placed guardrails all around her life so
the enemies could not take her out
To let the world know she belonged to Him;
of which there was no doubt.
Then, one day, God called to her and said, "I have
given you signs that you might have missed.
But my dear, sweet child Patty, you were born for times such as this.
For my sheep no longer hear my voice; they are wandering to and fro.
With no direction, with no purpose, with
no safe place where they can go.
So, I need you to go out on the highways, and
bi-ways, and the nursing homes too.
I will send you some faithful disciples to walk this journey with you.
But I need you to preach my gospel, don't deviate,
for my Word is already written
That I am the Alpha, and the Omega; and on the throne, I am sitting.*

*"Yes, sitting high and looking low, but I am with you all the way.
Don't worry about what man might try to do.
Don't worry about what they might say.
For your name is in the Book of Life; it is sealed with my approval.
It is not like the book of man, there is no chance for its removal.
For I knew you even before you were yet in your mother's womb,*

And I was with you during your hours of
bliss and hours of darkest gloom.
But through it all, your feet were planted on the Rock of my Salvation.
Which reflects your years of fasting, years of
praying, and years of dedication.
And so, my child, feed my sheep whether it is one or even thousands.
Whether they black or white, rich or poor, or
those who lack proper housings.
You have proven that you are battle-ready to lead the fight for me.
To bring the lost and the broken so that they too can be free.
And now, today, we all are witnesses of the outcome of God's call.
For it is twenty-five years and counting, and
Dr. Wright is still standing tall.
Her thirst for God has not diminished, if possible, it could be more.
As she waits to see what else El Shaddai has in store."

THE LETTER

I stumbled across an old book.
Its pages were yellowed and torn.
I searched for the cover,
And I found it was one that my grandmother owned.

The contents of the book
Included materials that was indiscreet.
But there was a prayer that was enclosed inside,
Penned in handwriting nice and neat.

IT READ:

Lord,

I'm not saved. But I heard that You hear sinners' prayers, too.
So, I have decided to take a moment to write one just for you.
My household is in chaos from my husband on down.
There is no one here that I can talk to, and no one else around.
I know my husband is running women. He has been doing it for many years,
But I have learned to keep quiet and swallow those unshed tears.
I had hoped that there would come a day He would finally see the light,
And come back to his family and try to make it right.
Our children have been scarred from all the abuse that they have seen.
But instead of comforting me, they have become nasty and mean.
Still, I try to encourage them to have hope, success, and to thrive.
But they have told me numerous times that they wish I were no longer alive.

Well, it seems they might get their wish for I am contemplating suicide.
If no one cares that I live, they darn sure do not care if I die.
But I heard suicide is unforgiveable. So, that is why I am torn.
How long must I suffer? How long do I keep holding on?
So, Lord if you see this prayer, send me a sign or two.
And show me what the heck a sinner like me is supposed to do.
I am so tired Lord. I am drained. Desperation has won the day.
I will be waiting for an answer. Lord, hear me now, I pray.

Wow, the letter was stunning.
I could not believe my eyes.
The way I remembered my grandmother.
This one caught me by surprise.

I *cried for all the pain*
That He had kept inside.
But then, as quickly as they sprung up,
The tears quickly dried.

For the grandmother that I knew
Was God-fearing indeed.
She always reminded me
That God will supply all our needs.

And my grandfather would say,
"Yep, God really cares."
So, you see, God did answer
my grandmother's prayer.

THE BATTERED WOMAN

I wandered through life
Drifting here and there
With little ambition
With few belongings and cares.
I bounced from wall to wall
In arms and out of them.
Sometimes, I've left unscathed,
Other times with battered limbs.

I put bandages over the cuts,
Gauzes over the pain,
Determined to battle on
So that I could feel whole again.
And when I often stumbled,
I searched for prying eyes
Who might have glimpsed my bruises
Who saw through my disguise.

Could they see my life was a façade?
A brave attempt at strength?
Who had a quest to be loved
That I pursued at any length?
It didn't matter there was pain
Or so I told myself
I just had to show the world
That I did not need anybody else.

For I have heard people talking,
How they wish they were more like me;
Happy and go-lucky,
young and carefree.
So, I must continue this quest;
Destination unknown,
Next time might be different,
Next time I won't feel so alone.

God's Responds (to the Battered Woman)

———•◆•———

I see the pain that you try to hide.
The cuts, the bruises, the tears you have cried.
The many hours that you have laid awake;
Tossing and turning with the tremors and shakes.

I see the mask that you have kept in place
To hide the agony on your face.
The barriers you have built are deep and wide
To safeguard the heart, and cling to your pride.

Most Important

I see the part no one else can see,
The lost child with all her vulnerabilities.
Your missteps you have made you carried like a cross,
Causing despair, desperation, and a feeling of loss.

So, I offer you hope and peace tonight
For my yoke is easy and my burden is light.
I will never forsake, no you will never be alone,
Until the day I carry you home.